THE BREAKDOWN
OF AUTHORITY

Gordon Talbot, Ph.D.

THE BREAKDOWN OF AUTHORITY

FLEMING H. REVELL COMPANY

Old Tappan, New Jersey

Scripture quotations in this volume are from the King James Version of the Bible.

Library of Congress Cataloging in Publication Data

Talbot, Gordon.
    The breakdown of authority.

    1. Authority.   2. Social   conflict.   3. Christian
ethics.   I. Title.
HM271.T24   248'.4   75-33052
ISBN 0-8007-0781-8

Contents

54323

Preface

Throughout history there have been periods in which authority has broken down in various parts of the world. However, such situations have seldom remained static for long. Authority of some kind has moved into these vacuums to bring about law and order again. Men are social creatures, and they demand rules and regulations to govern their relationships to one another.

Above the authority men generate among themselves is the Source of all authority, and this is God Himself. He is sovereign over all men, and they must all eventually reckon with Him, either in mercy or in judgment. The purpose of this book is to emphasize the need for divine authority in our world, whether it comes to us in a direct way, or is channeled to us through people God has delegated to represent His authority on the earth.

Christians cannot afford to let events just happen and show no concern for them. They must permeate society with scriptural teachings and actions. They should stand up and let the world hear what the Word of God has to say about society's problems. They need to work with individuals who lack the controlling power of God's Spirit in their lives. With compassion and love, they can help turn rebellious people into those who conform to God's will and seek the good of their fellowmen.

This is my attempt to stand up and be heard on a subject which is crying out for attention. Let credit be given to all the secular professionals wrestling with the problem, whenever they offer workable solutions — But let's not forget that the Scriptures have held the answers we seek for thousands of years.

—GORDON G. TALBOT

THE BREAKDOWN
OF AUTHORITY

1

Sources of Authority

Crime rates in the United States took a downward trend in 1972-73. In 1974 they started upward again, increasing a staggering 16 percent over the previous year. Criminals evidently decided to shift their operations to smaller, less well-protected areas. The rise was 6 percent in cities of one million or more, 19 percent in cities of 10,000-100,000, 25 percent in towns under 10,000, 21 percent in suburbs, and 19 percent in rural areas. These statistics represented only *reported* crimes, according to the 1975 *Reader's Digest Almanac,* from which these figures were taken. A large percentage of crimes always go unreported.

Problems of law enforcement have been aggravated by loss of respect for individuals in authority. A president

13

and vice-president resigned, each under his own cloud. Many were convicted for taking part in the Watergate scandal or its attempted cover-up. A Florida senator was indicted for extortion. A federal judge was the first of his kind sent to prison to serve a sentence for tax evasion and conspiracy — crimes perpetrated while he had been governor of Illinois. The chief county executive of Baltimore, who succeeded Spiro Agnew in that position, was sentenced for tax evasion, extortion, and conspiracy.

We *ought* to be alarmed by these developments. Not only is the quality of life lowered by the breakdown of authority, but the very existence of a nation is threatened by it. On the other hand, we should realize that such actions bring *re*actions, and people who demand law and order eventually get it in one form or another. Our concern should be that we get the right kinds. Let's discuss the three main types.

Divine Authority

Our powers of reasoning should convince every person that order exists within the universe and implies the existence of a supernatural Being. For every effect there has to be a cause. Since men did not bring the universe into existence, there must have been a greater Power who did. For every created thing there is evidence of design. Since men did not design created things, there must have been a greater Designer who did.

In addition to assumptions of Creation and design, we come to the subject of control. Does a supreme Being sustain the universe? If so, does He exercise control over it? There are people who think God created the universe and left it to run by its own laws without any interference by Him. Others think God takes a personal interest in all that happens in the universe and exercises sovereign control over all things.

The Holy Bible teaches the existence of a Triune God. God the Father, God the Son (Jesus Christ), and God the Holy Spirit were involved in the Creation of the universe, including this earth and everything on it. Genesis 1:1 tells us about the Father's part. Genesis 1:2 shows the Holy Spirit was involved. John 1:3, Colossians 1:16, and Hebrews 1:2 describe the Son's part.

The Holy Scriptures also teach that Jesus Christ sustains the universe, for ". . . by him all things consist" or hold together (Colossians 1:17). That answers the question as to whether a supreme Being sustains the universe. The Scriptures teach that God the Father ". . . hath committed all judgment unto the Son" (John 5:22). That answers the question as to whether a supreme Being exercises control over the universe.

Finally, the Bible teaches that God does indeed concern Himself with the universe, along with everyone and every thing on this earth. The Word of God is filled with illustrations of God's intervention in the affairs of men, either to bless or punish them. His authority has thus been demonstrated in both positive and negative ways. Prophecies indicate that His authority will continue to be exercised in the eternity stretching out before mankind. Those who yield to His will now are going to enjoy eternal blessing, but those who resist Him are going to suffer eternal condemnation.

Societal Authority

Since the creation of the human race in Adam and Eve, people have developed systems of authority among themselves, in order to promote law and order for the good of all. This was part of God's plan for exercising His authority on the earth. The Apostle Paul taught obedience to earthly authorities, whom he called "God's ministers" for praising the righteous and punishing the wicked (*see* Romans 13:1, 6, 7). The Apostle Peter agreed that civil authorities ought to be obeyed as a means of strengthening believers' testimonies among their fellowmen (*see* 1 Peter 2:13-17).

Both men obviously were thinking of authorities who were doing their jobs well, even though they might not be Christians. This is something to remember if you are pulled over by an officer for breaking the speed limit or becoming involved in any offense. In cases where the will of earthly authorities is contrary to the will of God,

Christians are obligated to follow the principle Peter laid down in Acts 5:29, "We ought to obey God rather than men."

Believers who choose to disobey earthly authorities on this basis have to be prepared to take the consequences of their actions. This may involve persecution from civil authorities, as it did for the early Christians, or as it did for Daniel when he continued to pray to God, in spite of the pagan emperor's order, and was cast into the lions' den. At such times, believers may claim the grace of God to sustain them until deliverance comes.

Authority in society can have a wide range of applications. In a totalitarian country, it may be vested in a dictator at the top. It has been reported that the president of one new African nation summons individuals who oppose his ideas to his office and personally administers beatings to them. In a democratic country, authority is vested in the people and delegated to officials at the local, state/provincial, and federal levels.

Authority in a modern democratic country is likely to be found in three categories: legislative, administrative and judicial. Those in each category are supposed to act as "checks and balances" to each other, so that none draws too much power to itself. When a free press is allowed to operate, responsible journalists can motivate the general public to demand wrongs in each branch of government be made right.

Pressures from government authorities and from society in general can become burdensome. As populations continue to increase and the pace of life gets even more frenzied than it now is, there are likely to be more and more regulations — written or unwritten — to plague us. We will be tempted to ignore them or rebel against them, but we must be careful to avoid doing anything which would hurt our Christian testimony. There are legitimate ways to handle our frustrations.

Personal Authority

A child's concept of authority is first learned at home. Here is where personal authority by the parents, live-in relatives, brothers, sisters, and baby-sitters is applied. The freewheeling youngster has a multitude of restrictions placed upon him as he learns the meaning of property rights and personal rights. He is taught to avoid hot things, sharp things, electrical shocks, dangerous heights, and various other threats to his health and happiness. He learns about keeping clean, dressing properly, eating in a mannerly way, and how to control his emotions with visitors and neighbors. He learns what is expected of him not only at home, but also at school, church, stores, or wherever he may go.

Until a child reaches the legal age of maturity, usually eighteen, he is under his parents' or guardians' authority. Even when he goes to school, the authority exercised by the administrators, teachers, and staff members over him is delegated to them by the parents or guardians. They can take him out of school at any time and send him to another school, or even teach him at home with tutors or by themselves, if they meet educational requirements laid down by the government. When he goes to the hospital, they can transfer him elsewhere, if they don't like the treatment he is getting. Only a court order, based on the child's welfare, could override their decision. He cannot get married without their consent.

As the child moves through the years of adolescence, he becomes more and more independent. Wise parents or guardians welcome this, and do all they can to help him develop the ability to take care of himself. By the time he reaches maturity he is ready to assume an adult's responsibilities — or should be.

What Romans 13:1-7 and 1 Peter 2:13-17 are to societal authority, Ephesians 5:22-6:4 and Colossians 3:18-21 are to family authority. Paul taught that God's plan is that the father should be the highest authority in the home, earning the love and respect of his wife and children by his wise and prayerful leadership. Wives are to be in submission to their husbands, and children are to be in submission to their parents, or to anyone placed over them by their parents.

There is no such thing as absolute freedom from authority. Divine authority operates regardless of what an individual thinks or does about it. Societal authority can hardly be avoided. Family authority is temporary but absolute while it is in force. We must learn to live within the framework of authority, realizing it does have benefits.

2

Causes of Rebellion

The world seems to be made up of manipulators and the manipulated. Sometimes the same person plays both roles, being manipulated by those above him and manipulating in turn those below him. When people rebel against those in authority, they usually do so because of frustration and an opportunity to find relief.

Rebellion or revolution are terms which conjure up very negative thoughts and feelings. We remember the bloody battles of history which were motivated by hatred and greed. We think of those who have rebelled against God and paid a bitter price for it.

However, there have been times when changes from the status quo could no longer be denied. In such situations, revolutionaries were called heroes and patriots by

those who felt their cause was just. The important thing
for Christians to decide in each case involving their loyal-
ties was whether the cause and the means for accomplish-
ing it were approved by the Lord.

Our primary aim in this chapter is to analyze the
reasons why individuals rebel. However, certain value
judgments on the rightness or wrongness of rebellion are
bound to creep in. The last part of the chapter may not
be well received by pacifists, but it is hoped they will
be gracious about another view.

Selfish Interests

Resistance to authority is a fact of life. One of the most
common reasons is a desire to satisfy selfish interests. It
is easy to note that little children just naturally look out
for themselves. They want what they want when they
want it, and they will go to great lengths to get it. Complaining, crying, and even temper tantrums are in their
arsenal of psychological weapons to use on parents.

Children who are older learn new techniques. They
may compare their miserable lives to the wonderful lives
lived by their friends, whose parents are supposedly more
understanding, fair, and flexible than their own. They
may indulge in black moods over extended periods of
time. They may be deliberately disobedient in order to
"punish" and frustrate their parents.

As we look at displays of selfishness in children, we realize that this juvenile trait remains unconquered in many young people — and adults, as well. People will lie, cheat, steal, assault, murder, and even start riots or wars because of selfish greed. They care nothing for the property, health, feelings, or even lives of others, so long as they get what they want. Authorities who get in their way run the risk of being cut down.

The Apostle Paul described selfish people as being fleshly minded or carnally minded. "For they that are after the flesh do mind the things of the flesh; but they that are after the Spirit the things of the Spirit. For to be carnally minded is death; but to be spiritually minded is life and peace. Because the carnal mind is enmity against God: for it is not subject to the law of God, neither indeed can be" (Romans 8:5-7). Therefore, we would do well to call selfishness an expression of man's sinful nature and deal with it on a spiritual level.

Natural Assertion

Rebellion can be motivated by natural assertion on the part of an individual, especially one who is young and developing a spirit of independence. (This was mentioned briefly when considering the shifting of authority from parents to sons or daughters who are approaching maturity.) It is a trait that is most discernible among young people in their teens.

A mother bear watches over her cubs very carefully for two entire years. However, as she prepares for a new litter, she ignores the two-year-olds and even chases them away. The time has come for them to be on their own, and they soon adapt to the situation and succeed in caring for themselves.

In some cultures, men release their hold on their children at a much younger age than in the more highly advanced cultures. By the time a boy or girl completes the initiation rites upon entering puberty, he or she becomes a full-fledged adult member of the tribe. The demands of civilization have caused us to prolong the period of dependence for our children. We don't feel they are mentally, emotionally, or economically ready to enter the adult world until they are close to twenty years of age, and if they plan on college work and graduate work they may be well into their twenties before we feel they are ready.

We have created a subculture, called *adolescence*, which may last from twelve through twenty-four. During those twelve years, young people are expected to live under our authority, just as they did the first twelve years of their lives. What some adults fail to realize is that the natural drive toward independence is going to assert itself during this period and demand to be recognized and given its rightful place in their development.

A parallel is found in young nations, seeking to emerge

from years of colonial rule. Following World War II, scores of colonies gained their independence and took their place in the world of nations. In many cases, the results were deplorable, because the colonial "parents" had not trained the colonial people to take care of themselves. Sometimes anarchy took over, and many innocent people died. Economies teetered on the brink of bankruptcy. The superpowers rushed in to establish their influence, and a new form of "colonialism" took the place of the old. Authority of one sort or another seeks a vacuum and occupies it.

Rebellion — if it is exerted in order to claim the natural right to independence — and if it is done in legitimate ways — can be a positive force. Authorities have to learn how to guide it so that those involved will profit from it and not harmfully disrupt their lives.

External Oppression

Rebellion may be motivated by inner selfishness or inner desire to assert independence, but external oppression can also cause it. Literal slavery may be rare in our day (except in slave-labor camps housing political prisoners in various nations), but there are other forms of slavery in existence.

There is political oppression in many parts of the world, especially those under Communist rule or influence. There is economic oppression which keeps millions in hopeless poverty. There is military oppression, with flare-ups occurring all over the globe, in spite of the best efforts of peace-oriented diplomats. One of the most vicious and senseless types of military oppression is found in terrorist activities, for many innocent people become the victims of brutal actions.

There is something deep within the human mind and personality which will not remain permanently placid while others exert unbearable pressures from outside. Experts have tried fanatically to break the human will — sometimes succeeding but other times inexplicably failing. When oppression reaches its saturation point, and an opportunity to change things presents itself, or can be devised — watch out! People are going to stand up and fight back.

The Apostle Paul wrote, "If it be possible, as much as lieth in you, live peaceably with all men" (Romans 12:18). The main thrust of the verse is in favor of peace, but the implication is clear that there may be times when peace is unattainable in human affairs. In some situations the Lord will do the fighting, as He did when He delivered the Israelites through the Red Sea and then slew their enemies in the same waters (*see* Exodus 14:21-30). In other situations the Lord requires His people to fight back, as He did when the Israelites met the Amalekites in battle at Rephidim not long afterward (*see* Exodus 17:8-13).

Paul said, "For the weapons of our warfare are not carnal, but mighty through God to the pulling down of strong holds" (2 Corinthians 10:4). This is certainly true when we are engaged in spiritual battles. However, that text should not be used to support the belief that literal warfare is always avoidable. Something concrete must be done by righteous men to keep thugs from taking over the world. If they fail to use their strength to help the oppressed, God will hold them accountable for inaction.

What is true among nations and large groups is also true for individuals. God may require us to be deeply humiliated and suffer persecution at times. He may also require us to serve as "powers . . . ordained of God" to be "ministers of God" for praising the righteous and punishing the wicked (*see* Romans 13:1-7). This is not an endorsement for vigilante action. We will have to follow the leading of the Holy Spirit explicitly, rising to positions of leadership only in legitimate ways and determining to serve others rather than ourselves.

Many fine Christian people have had to make the agonizing decision in centuries past as to whether or not to give all they had in order to deliver themselves, their loved ones, and others from external oppression. They chose to do so, and they preserved freedom for generations to come. We may be faced with the same challenge in our day, and we ought to be ready to do what we know is right.

3

Blessings of Conformity

When the Viet Cong took control of Saigon in the spring of 1975, there were no reports of immediate reprisals. Reeducation courses, which lasted three months, were set up for senior military officers of the former pro-American regime. The impression left by the Communists was that their regime might be the most tolerant in Asia. They were appealing to the desire in the hearts of most people that there would be peace in their lives after thirty years of warfare.

Under most governments there are promises of a good life, if people will conform to what leaders require. It is in this sense, then, that we now discuss the blessings of conformity. We are no: trying to make value judgments as to which types of government are good or bad (although we naturally prefer democracy for ourselves, and we wish people in all lands could have it, too).

When the Apostle Paul wrote Romans 13:1-7, and when the Apostle Peter wrote 1 Peter 2:13-17, the Roman Empire ruled Palestine. In spite of pagan control, these men of God urged believers to conform to governmental requirements. They obviously spoke as if authorities were doing their jobs well, although they knew such authorities were not perfect. The basic concept they presented was that government itself is good, and anarchy is bad. They wanted Christians to be exemplary citizens wherever they lived.

Sense of Security

Now we want to emphasize the blessings of conformity on a *personal* level. Later we will pay more attention to the blessings of conformity on the *societal* level, stressing the values of law and order.

Conformity to the authority of Christ is the most important kind of conformity a person can have. We may wonder sometimes if earthly authorities are always right, and if they always act in our best interests, but we never have to worry about that with Christ. He makes no mistakes, and He always wants the best for us.

Christ made it very plain that conformity to Him must be based upon love. He told His followers, "If ye love me, keep my commandments" (John 14:15). Those who do this become increasingly like Him. They come to realize that nothing can separate them from His love, whether it is in the natural or supernatural realms. Such a strong bond is forged between them and Christ that they feel secure in Him (*see* Romans 8:35-39). They can be "stedfast, unmoveable, always abounding in the work of the Lord. . ." (1 Corinthians 15:58).

A sense of security develops between individuals and those who have jurisdiction over them on earth, such as parents, teachers, employers, officials, physicians, and others. In spite of all the talk about individuals wanting to "do their own thing," there are many times when they appreciate and even place themselves voluntarily under the authority of others, so they might gain the sense of security it brings.

As an illustration, think of a young man who is graduated from college and is accepted for a management-training position with a large corporation. He moves into this new experience conditioned to the fact that if he does as he is told, and if he is creative and imaginative when it counts, he can look forward to a secure future with the corporation in the years ahead. He may be disappointed in time, but he starts out with a sense of security, and that grows as he gains confidence in the corporation.

Sense of Tranquility

There are people who believe in "peace at any price," meaning they consider tranquility more important than anything else. On the surface, their goal seems faultless. Many references in the Bible urge men to seek peace. However, God never meant for people to "sell their souls" in order to obtain peace.

It was thinking such as that which spawned the slogan stating "I would rather be red than dead." This had reference to those who would choose to live under communism than to die in an attempt to remain free. Millions have had to make this decision in recent years, and millions more will be faced with it, if communism continues its steady advance in the world.

The only kind of peace and tranquility we are certain will never boomerang on us is that which Christ gives us. He said, "Peace I leave with you, my peace I give unto you: not as the world giveth, give I unto you. Let not your heart be troubled, neither let it be afraid" (John 14:27). Paul told the Philippians, "Be careful [anxious] for nothing; but in every thing by prayer and supplication with thanksgiving let your requests be made known unto God. And the peace of God, which passeth all understanding, shall keep your hearts and minds through Christ Jesus" (Philippians 4:6, 7).

Conformity to Christ does not necessarily provide

peace without problems. It does provide peace in the midst of problems. An artist once won an art contest on the theme of peace by painting a raging storm on a seacoast. It was an unlikely scene, but on looking closely a tiny bird could be observed in a dry niche in the rocks, singing for all it was worth! So it is with the Christian who puts his trust in Christ regardless of circumstances.

The chronic rebel cannot hope to have much peace and tranquility, for his constant attempts to stir things up against the status quo will generate more heat than light in most cases. There are definitely times when the status quo needs to be changed, but the process is bound to bring upheaval. That's why it is extremely important that we are absolutely convinced of a need for change — and that God is leading us to make the change — before we involve ourselves in any kind of revolutionary action. We must remember that *the ends* do not always justify *the means*.

Sense of Unity

Conformity to common belief and practice can help develop a sense of strong unity within a group, and that can be a great blessing to all involved. A group torn by factions is a reproach to its people and the cause it claims to embrace. This is nowhere more true than in the church. Paul was very sad about the situation in the church at

Corinth, when it was reported to him by members of the house of Chloe. He wrote to the believers there, and pleaded with them to heal their divisions and try to pull together (*see* 1 Corinthians 1:10-17; 3:1-10).

In writing to the believers in Philippi, Paul told them that his spiritual goal in life was to be conformed to Christ. Realizing some of his readers might not agree with him, Paul said, "Let us therefore, as many as be perfect, be thus minded: and if in any thing ye be otherwise minded, God shall reveal even this unto you" (Philippians 3:15). In other words, he believed that unity had to be based on God's working in the hearts of individuals, and that sometimes proceeds at different paces among them. Eventually, all believers led by the Spirit of God will come to unanimous conclusions.

In deciding whether or not the Gentile believers would have to keep the Mosaic law, the church council in Jerusalem discussed it at length, and then James announced, "For it seemed good to the Holy Ghost, and to us, to lay upon you [Gentiles] no greater burden than these necessary things . . ." and he then listed four things such converts should avoid, so as not to offend pious Jews living among them (*see* Acts 15:28, 29).

God has a definite chain of command in mind for members of Christian families. Paul outlined this in Ephesians 5:22-6:4 and in Colossians 3:18-21. He knew this would be necessary in order for unity to prevail in the home. The father was to be the head of the family, who firmly but lovingly led the rest. Children were to be obedient to parents, and, by inference, to anyone placed over them by their parents. This pattern has been disregarded in many homes, and trouble occurs to mar the unity of the families.

Even in a one-to-one relationship between two persons, there has to be some measure of conformity if there is to be unity. That doesn't mean an individual has to lose his or her personal identity or never have any difference of opinion with the other person, but it does mean the two have to be in agreement on basic things, if they are to walk together through life. God asked the Israelites, "Can two walk together, except they be agreed?" (Amos 3:3), and the answer was obviously that they could not. Unity is a blessing, and disunity is a curse.

Western culture has been noted for its emphasis on individualism. Many other cultures, both primitive and advanced, have put an emphasis on conformity to the ideals of extended families or community groupings. Who can say which is better, for the bases of evaluation will vary. The flexibility and independence allowed by the western way of life are things few who have them would want to give up, and yet those who visit or take up residence in foreign cultures are often amazed by the benefits of conformity found among such people.

Conformity to Christ spans all cultures. As individuals draw closer to Him, they automatically draw closer to one another. Here is the basis for fellowship among Christians. ". . . truly our fellowship is with the Father, and with his Son Jesus Christ" (1 John 1:3).

4

Dangers of Nonconformity

Perhaps nowhere is the need for conformity greater than in a correctional facility. The New York State Division for Youth's School, located on 1,500 unfenced acres at upstate Industry (near Rochester), is the oldest of its kind in the United States. Criticism was heard in 1975 that too much permissiveness, idleness, and emphasis on recreation was leading to increasing threats, acts of violence, and escapes among the institution's 220 boys. Some felt it was a powder keg ready to blow up at any time, perhaps leading to a revolt similar to the one which occurred at Attica not far away in 1971.

Whenever authority breaks down, nonconformity flourishes, and dangers develop. The more unstable the persons involved, the greater the dangers become. Psychologists, sociologists, and criminologists who like to experiment with loosened controls should be held responsible when those experiments lead to undermining of authority and deterioration of situations such as that at Industry.

We don't have to limit our thinking to institutions. Even on the individual level, nonconformity can be fraught with dangers. These include development of inner emotional turmoils, serious conflicts of interest with others, and even traumatic personal rejections by individuals or society in general.

Inner Turmoils

The nonconformist may pay a high price for deviant behavior, whether he is right or wrong in what he thinks or does. Whether he "marches to the beat of another drum" out of inner conviction, a desire to focus attention on himself, or for some other reason, he should reckon with the fact that his nonconformity can lead to unpleasant repercussions both inside and outside himself. He may literally place his health, happiness and life itself in danger.

This is not intended to squelch all nonconformists. There may be situations in which nonconformity is exactly what is needed. If that is the case, then dangers cannot be the deciding factor as to whether a person acts or not. He should act, regardless of the dangers involved. However, if a person is not strongly motivated to act in a nonconformist way, then he should be aware of the fact that deviant behavior can lead to harm, and reckless self-endangerment or the endangerment of others is certainly to be avoided.

Anyone who goes against the normal pattern of things runs the risk of developing inner turmoils, which can hurt his emotional and even his physical health. There is within every individual a desire to belong to individuals and groups he considers important. We will consider this in more detail later, but it should be mentioned here that failure to succeed in being accepted by those he considers important can lead to inner stress.

Most people have a yearning to get along with their associates, although their relationships may range from casual to intimate. When something happens to disrupt a relationship, blame is usually placed, and it most often is directed toward the nonconformist. This can cause him to suffer emotional strain, and he will try to cope with it the best way he can. If he is successful, and the relationship gets back on the track, he will breathe a sigh of relief and go on as before. However, if he fails to cope successfully with it, he may try desperate measures to handle it, or he may cut off the relationship altogether. In either case, he may be branded a misfit, compounding his problem.

This can also lead to physical ailments. Physicians have strongly asserted for a long time now that many patients who visit them have ailments caused by emotional stress. Headaches, stomach disorders, ulcers, heart troubles, sexual problems, and perhaps even arthritis can be traced to such emotions as fear, anger, and hatred. Not all nonconformists are motivated by such emotions but some undoubtedly are.

Conflicting Interests

An individual who goes his way, while others go in other directions, will find what happens inside himself important. The manner in which he affects other people will be important, too, for they will react in ways which can make him happy or sad. He may claim he doesn't care what people think of him, but chances are he really does care.

Teenagers, within their own subculture, are probably the most socially conscious of all age groups. Peer pressure can be very strong at this stage of their lives. Conformity is shown in habits of grooming, dress, speech, attitudes, and various other things. Nonconformity can have opposite effects. If a teenage leader decides to go from long hair to short hair, or initiate any other kind of change from the prevailing norm, he may create a new norm for others to follow. However, if a nonleader decides to do the same thing, he may be subjected to ridicule and ostracized.

As far as adults are concerned, a strongly conservative person working in a social services department of a municipal government may find himself at odds every day with liberally oriented co-workers. While he insists on tightening up controls on freeloaders, who could work but who refuse, he discovers his colleagues sidestepping the controls mandated by law and allowing their case loads to proliferate. He can stay and fight the battle alone, he can report the situation to higher authorities, or he can quit his job. Whatever happens, his nonconformity exacts a high price.

Nonconformists who have received the most publicity in recent years have been those banded together for the purpose of protesting various things they opposed in society. Labled *radicals* by others, they have agitated for civil rights, an end to the war in Vietnam, and various other causes. Conflicts of interest between them and the general population led to scoffing, acts of violence, full-scale rioting, legislative changes, and even acceptance of their views by the majority of people in the end.

It was a small but well-organized and dedicated group of Marxists who staged the Russian Revolution in 1917. Communists now control half the world's people and influence many others. Christians, and others in the free world who want to preserve liberty, will have to be as organized and dedicated, if they hope to counteract the menace. The point being made here is that nonconformists cannot simply be written off, for they often wield power far out of proportion to their numbers, if once they are united.

Personal Rejections

Let's come back now to the plight of the one nonconformist who persists in charting his own course in defiance of what others around him are doing. Once he goes beyond the tolerable limits of deviant behavior — however that may be defined by those associated with him — the danger of rejection by them increases each time he makes contact with them.

Circumstances determine the intensity of that rejection. A person who walks around town backwards may be considered strange or mentally unbalanced, but he could conceivably do it for years without interference. However, a person attempting to drive an automobile around town backwards would probably get only a few blocks before he was arrested and perhaps fined for endangering others.

Consider two diverse job applicants at a factory: One, a school dropout, is hired, and then is soon fired because he cannot get along well with other employees. He may drift from job to job, feeling rejected, but taking it in stride and blaming himself for lack of education. Another is a college teacher with a Ph.D., who falsifies his application so he can be hired. He wants to work with his hands among common people for a change, because he is tired of the classroom. When his true identity is discovered, he, too, is fired. The stated reason is that he falsified his application, but the real reason is that his employer considers him overqualified and likely to quit after being trained for his factory job. Such rejection may be felt intensely by this man, for he feels more locked into one line of work even than the school dropout is, and he is more sensitive to rejection.

Modern society has created some special stresses and strains all its own. By the time a person is forty years old, he has to be fairly well settled into his vocation, because no one wants to retrain him for another line of work. At the same time, automation is putting people out of work, so they must learn new skills. An individual may want to conform to remaining at his normal occupation, and yet find it impossible to do so. He becomes an unwilling nonconformist, and that can be miserable.

The time to be experimental and nonconformist would appear to be in one's youth. There is a natural trend toward conservatism within most adults as they grow older. Society will tolerate and perhaps be amused by the offbeat attitudes and actions of the young, but it has little patience with the mature who indulge in them.

As mentioned earlier, there may be times when nonconformity is exactly what is needed in certain situations. However, the nonconformist should count the cost and be aware of the dangers involved when he refuses to do what is expected of him by others.

5

Needs of Individuals

On May 10, 1975, the Police Benevolent Association took out a full-page ad in the Buffalo *Evening News*. It was headlined DO YOU WANT THE BATTLE AGAINST CRIME TO STOP IN BUFFALO? Then followed these items:

> - **Your chance of becoming a victim of crime has doubled in just ten years.**
> - **Your chance of becoming a victim of a violent crime has increased by more than five times in this same period.**
> - **Today you have a 1 in 20 chance of being a victim of any crime.**
> - **Today you have a 1 in 100 chance of being a victim of a violent offense.**

An appeal was then made to contact one's local councilman at city hall and ask for an adequate budget to support the police force in Buffalo.

The motivation behind that ad was, of course, to stir within the general public a desire to call for security in a society plagued by rising crime rates. *The desire for security* is a basic psychological drive in every person.

50

Security is one aspect of the need to belong to a society in which one does not feel threatened. Another need people have is *affection,* meaning the opportunity to love others and be loved in return. A third is the *need for new experiences in life* — something different from the regular routine.

The reason we are going to consider these needs here is that individuals will seek to satisfy these basic drives, and if authorities try to stop them, they may resist. Thus, situations can occur in which a breakdown of authority takes place. We must understand the implications of this, if we are to understand how authority breaks down.

Belonging

We could hardly avoid discussing the matter of belonging when we dealt previously with the blessings of conformity and the dangers of nonconformity. Let's look into it more deeply here, especially as it applies to single individuals.

Moving from one town to another is difficult for families, and millions of them have to do it each year. Teenagers are particularly unhappy about the necessity for adjusting to new situations. Going into a new high school, they have to get used to new teachers, make new friends, and fit into new customs and schedules.

Suppose a teenager is very shy, has a handicap, or

finds it nearly impossible to make or keep friends. He has left his former home, school, church, and set routine, only to discover he is held at arm's length in the new location. He will suffer from a lack of belonging. As a consequence, he may go to classes late in order to avoid crowded hallways. He may become irritable and quarrel with others over minor things. He may become a chronic complainer. He is sending out signals for help, but authorities may consider him simply a troublemaker. Sensitive administrators, counselors, teachers, and students will see his problem and try to help him make a good adjustment.

Suppose a man has worked long and hard for his company, only to have another employee with less seniority and experience promoted ahead of him. He may turn sour, slack off on the job, and even contemplate subtle forms of sabotaging the company's business. An insensitive employer might fire him, but an understanding one would anticipate his feelings and try to provide other forms of compensation to offset his disappointment regarding being passed over for promotion. In this way, the employer can make him feel he still belongs and thus retain his loyalty to the company.

A woman may think she has a good marriage at first, only to discover as the years go by that her husband is an incipient tyrant. He makes demands rather than suggestions, and causes her to feel she is more of a servant than a partner. She may draw into a protective shell and find various ways to avoid following his leadership. It is hoped that he will become aware of his problem, and do something about it before it is too late.

Affection

A second need every individual has is to love and be loved. This is not always an intense or intimate kind of love, for it may be simply a casual relationship with others whom he knows but with whom he actually has little to do. At one end of the spectrum may be a very close relationship with his wife and children. At the other end may be only a smile and a hello for a fellow bus rider on the way to work. In between will be a wide range of relationships in which he feels the need to be pleasant toward others, and to have them reciprocate by being pleasant toward him.

Although it may be true that some individuals give much more love than they ever receive, the equation seems to have a way of leveling out over the long run. In other words, love generates love. When it is given, it has a tendency to come back. "Cast thy bread upon the waters: for thou shalt find it after many days" (Ecclesiastes 11:1).

A person who wants people to like him may become frustrated because no one seems to appreciate him. In his frustration, he may manifest some of the same traits shown by the one who wants to belong to a group but gets frozen out, as noted earlier. Fraternal bonds among outcasts of society are not at all uncommon, as shown by the close relationships formed between prisoners. Many individuals have been drawn into revolutionary groups because of the attention they received, even though they may realize those groups are using them for their own selfish purposes. Countless individuals have moved outside the bounds of law and order in a search for love, no matter how perverted it may be.

An assembly of Christians is nothing, if it fails to provide individuals with opportunities for righteous fellowship. If it is only a collection of people who are doctrinally correct, it lacks the vital element of love God planned it should have. When a church becomes cold and unloving, it is on its way toward developing into just another organization, rather than being a living organism with Christ as its Head (*see* Ephesians 1:22, 23). Its leaders should not be surprised if no one wants to submit to its authority. It is only as they act as the loving Christ acts that they have the right to exercise their authority in the church.

Experiences

A third need every individual has is *to have new experiences in life*. Just as the physical body needs to move and exercise its muscles, so the psychological part of a person needs to think new thoughts and feel new emotions. Routine is fine when it comes to developing a sense of security and belonging, but it is the periodic changes in life-style which make life interesting. Deprive a person of new experiences, and he may push against your authority in an effort to get them.

Individuals vary in their capacity for new experiences and their enjoyment of them. Some are perfectly content to hold down boring jobs and spend their spare hours in normal pursuits fifty weeks a year, but then they get away from it all for two-week vacations featuring entirely different life-styles. Others have to have something new happening to them practically every day, or they get very restless.

It is likely that people who want variety and challenging experiences seek out vocations which supply excitement — police work, professional athletics, military service, politics, rescue-squad work, and others. They thrive on fast-moving actions and solving problems. Put them in a dull, routine, boring line of work, and they would be unhappy. These people would be miserable, and possibly even dangerous, if they were to be placed under a totalitarian system which restricted them to boring jobs and after-hours activities.

Some individuals may be hyperactive because of body metabolism. Others may have inherited certain excitable traits. Still others may seek a multitude of new experiences because of influence of environment, or relatives and friends who prize that kind of life. Some are imbued with a great idea or cause which mobilizes them and changes their whole way of life. The Apostle Paul was on his way to becoming another stuffy Pharisee when he was converted to Christ and became the church's greatest missionary of the first century, filling his life with a long list of exciting adventures.

Any of us who serve in places of leadership over others will have to reckon with the need for new experiences in those we serve. If we fail to do this, we will soon learn that our authority will be put to the test over and over again. In other words, we must be flexible enough to make allowances for those under our jurisdiction who are naturally creative and curious, seeking out new experiences continually. They cannot be expected to fit into preconceived molds and stay there.

We have seen that every individual has a basic drive to want to belong to individuals and groups he considers important to himself, to both give and receive affection, and to have opportunity for new experiences. We cannot fight against these God-given psychological drives and expect our authority to go unchallenged. We must learn to channel these drives into legitimate and Christ-honoring activities.

6

Types of Motivation

Daniel Boone, an outstanding figure in American history, dearly loved frontier life. While other men huddled in towns, cities, and neighboring farms along the Atlantic Seaboard, Boone was busy opening up the wilderness of Kentucky to settlers. He thought living close to nature was the next best thing to heaven itself. One day a group of hunters, going through deep woods, heard an outrageous sound. They crept up to it, expecting to find some new beast, but they found Boone sprawled on the ground and singing at the top of his voice for pure joy. He found value in a way of life some men would despise.

No one does anything without some kind of motive. This is extremely important in our consideration of the subject of authority. If we want people to obey authority, we will have to convince them to obey it for some reason they consider worthwhile. We may motivate them by using threats or punishments. We may lure them with prizes and various forms of recognition. We may persuade them there is value and permanence in doing what we want. Obviously, the last mentioned is by far the best type of motivation we could use.

It should be significant to us that God never forces a person to make spiritual advances in his life. Only those steps which are voluntary are considered valid with the Lord. There may be times when men have to use force with those who are incorrigible, but our goal ought to be voluntary decisions and actions on the part of those for whom we are responsible.

Threat and Punishment

The lowest forms of motivation have to be threat and punishment. They are mentioned together, because the first without the second is useless. In other words, it does no good to threaten punishment unless there is a determination to follow through if the threat is ignored. Threat and punishment are often used with little children, because they seem to require correction many times a day, and any other method would take too long or cost too much to implement. The life of a mother of young children can be very exhausting for this reason.

Threat and punishment are also used extensively in connection with inmates of correctional institutions, or those released on parole. They play a large part in basic training programs for military servicemen. In totalitarian countries they are commonly used for a wide variety of purposes to keep the people in line with leaders' wishes.

There are liberals who would like to do away with all forms of threat and punishment, considering them degrading and brutalizing, and, therefore, contrary to good psychology. Conservatives, on the other hand, realize there is a place for their use, especially with individuals who cannot seem to understand more sophisticated forms of motivation to conform to what society requires of them. The battle between liberals and conservatives on this matter will probably always be with us.

Sinful human nature being what it is, we have to consider it in our decision whether or not to use threat and punishment. The Bible is filled with divine warnings to sinful men. It is also filled with accounts of divine punishments for infractions of God's regulations. Do men dare to completely eliminate threats and punishments, concluding they are more adept at motivating people than God Himself is?

Romans 13:3, 4 makes it clear that the Lord sanctions the use of force in cases where people are evil and become menaces to society.

> For rulers are not a terror to good works, but to the evil. . . . For he [a ruler] is the minister of God to thee for good. But if thou do that which is evil, be afraid; for he beareth not the sword in vain: for he is the minister of God, a revenger to execute wrath upon him that doeth evil.

Prize and Recognition

Another step up the scale of motivation techniques is that of prize and recognition. The only difference between the two is that a prize is something tangible, while recognition is usually intangible. However, there may be times when prize and recognition are combined. If possible, it is better to award prizes or recognitions to honor individuals for doing things from a higher motive than that of merely to obtain those prizes or recognitions.

For example, we would not think much of a person who went out to rescue someone from a raging flood simply because he wanted to earn a thousand dollars and get his picture in the newspaper. However, if he rescued someone for humanitarian reasons, we would think it proper for him to be awarded a citation for heroism, get a picture and write-up in the newspaper, and perhaps even a monetary award.

Authorities sometimes use prizes and publicity in attempts to get their policies implemented. Rewards will be offered for apprehension of criminals, or information leading to their arrest. Blue-ribbon citizens committees will be set up to deal with special problems, and it is considered a great honor to be chosen to such committees. City or town councils will prepare tax write-offs, and perhaps install utilities for newly developed industrial parks, in order to lure new corporations into their communities. There are various other incentives used in the business world.

The use of prizes and recognitions for students in educational systems raises a problem which should be considered carefully. Is it a good idea to "pay" students to study or to behave properly? Many would argue against that kind of motivation, while others would accept it. It would seem that extensive use of this technique could get out of hand eventually, so it would appear wise to limit it.

The use of prizes and recognitions in the church's educational program may be even more sensitive, because we ought not to "pay" students to study the Bible, invite others to church, or make any kind of spiritual advance. Our whole purpose in that setting should be to convince students that God's Word is valuable to them on its own merits and does not require artificial means of enhancement.

Value and Permanence

We come now to the best form of motivation, regardless of the kind of setting involved. If we can convince people that doing something we want them to do is valuable to them and will have permanent effect on their lives, we are well on our way to motivating them to do it. Here is where we *ought* to start with them, and we should go down the scale to prizes, recognitions, threats, and punishments only if we are unsuccessful at the highest level. This will demand much preparation and patience on our part.

Authorities in totalitarian systems often get the notion they exist to be served by the people under them. Authorities in democratic systems are supposed to think of themselves as existing to serve the people who elected them to office. However, sometimes elected officials, or those appointed to their positions by elected officials, forget or overlook this fact and begin to act in a totalitarian manner themselves. They will ride roughshod over the people, using threats and punishments to accomplish what ought to be accomplished by democratic means. Fortunately, action at the ballot boxes and the operation of a free press usually weed out such individuals in time.

People who have a minimum of common sense, and who are well informed, normally arrive at the truth regarding situations eventually. Those who have studied God's Word and are aware of His dealings with men have to admit that His authority is absolute, and it is applied in beneficial ways to those who adhere to it. The longer they walk with God, the more valuable they find their relationship with Him to be. Earthly authorities are by no means perfect, but if they conscientiously seek to do their work well, people develop confidence in them, too.

Whether we are trying to get a seemingly incorrigible

juvenile delinquent to obey the law, or persuade a child to get to bed and have a good night's sleep, our approach should begin with convincing him of the value of such action to himself. It is not that we are trying to appeal strictly to selfishness, but we must realize that motivation is best when it comes from within a person, rather than being imposed from outside. There is really no substitute for self-discipline. Inner authority is superior to outer authority. (This subject will be treated more thoroughly when we consider controls.)

Sometimes our authority must be used to persuade individuals of the permanent value of actions which appear to have temporary drawbacks. For example, if a person needs surgery to correct a condition which will limit his activities all his life if left unattended, we may have to persuade him to go through the temporary pain, discomfort, and disruption of routine involved.

We have just seen that various forms of motivation may be used to try to get people to do what we want them to do. By far the best type of motivation is value and permanence, and that is where we should always start, if possible. If we have to go down the line to prize and recognition or to threat and punishment, at least we can be satisfied we began with the best, and went to the others only when it was apparent those under our care were not ready for the best.

7

Kinds of Disorders

When things pile up, problems occur. After the fall of Cambodia and South Vietnam to the Communists, over $50 million worth of food and machines being shipped to Southeast Asia by the United States began to pile up in Asian warehouses. The Agency for International Development slapped a stop order on shipments and took action to claim the goods as still belonging to the United States. However, the nations storing the goods threatened to take possession of them, since they planned to recognize the new Communist regimes and did not want to antagonize them. Thus, once again, another monstrous problem developed in that unfortunate corner of the world.

Sometimes things pile up on a personal basis, too, so

that an individual faces problems he cannot seem to handle. We will consider the three main kinds of disorders which develop — *maladjustments, neuroses,* and *psychoses.* As a person tries to cope with failure to satisfy his basic physical and psychological needs, his frustration mounts. If he is like most people, he will make a proper adjustment by himself or with help from relatives and friends. However, there is always the possibility he will make a bad adjustment or go beyond to a neurotic or psychotic state which will require professional help.

The relevance of all of this to behavior under a system of authority should be obvious. We can expect personal disorders to affect an individual's relationship to those in authority over him. Negative behavior may range from mild irritation to violent action or from rational to irrational conduct.

Everyday Maladjustments

A person uses several techniques to cope with everyday problems. He may not even be aware of their names or the fact that people all around him are using them, too. In some cases, these techniques can be either good or bad in nature. For example, compromise can go in both directions. Some techniques are definitely bad, such as regressing to childhood behavior demonstrates immaturity and creates its own problems. Let's consider the eight basic maladjustments individuals often make as they seek to cope with life.

First, they use *rationalization.* They attribute their actions to reasonable and believable motives, without adequately analyzing their true motives. For example, they may cheat on their income tax, and excuse it by saying, "Everyone does it!" They are being dishonest, but they convince themselves they are being sufficiently honest. Authorities may have to audit their returns to discover their cheating.

Second, they use *compensation* or *substitution.* They put something in place of that which is unacceptable or unattainable. For example, they may not qualify for visas into a foreign country, so they buy false visas from an illegitimate source. Immigration officials have to investigate and catch them.

Third, they use *identification.* They pattern themselves after people they greatly admire. For example, they may pour out adulation on outstanding political leaders, only to discover they are corrupt. Because of this, they no longer trust any government leaders.

Fourth, they use *compromise.* They settle an argument by making mutual concessions with others. For example, they may go with friends to sinful activities with the understanding their friends will come with them to church activities. The pastor hears of it and has to exhort them to do only what is righteous.

Fifth, they use *repression.* They push unacceptable desires or impulses into their subconsciousness and leave them there to operate. For example, they may fail to make restitution for offenses perpetrated before they were converted to Christ, and this robs them of victory in their spiritual development. They will have to obey God and get those things straightened out, if they want to be victorious Christians.

Sixth, they use *regression.* They return to earlier stages of development. For example, they may be easily hurt if they attempt to do jobs in the church which don't turn out well. Church leaders have to constantly bolster them with lavish praise to keep them going, as one would with a child.

Seventh, they use *withdrawal.* They prefer to fantasize, rather than face reality. For example, they may apply for positions at certain companies and then broadcast it as fact they are going to work there, only to be notified they were not accepted. This can be embarrassing both for them and the company officials involved.

Eighth, they use *negativism* or *egocentrism.* They refuse to do anything but what benefits themselves.

For example, they would do favors for rich people, because they might get something back, but they would not do anything for poor people who cannot repay them. God has to show them this is contrary to Christian ethics.

Neurotic Changes

If a person persists in making bad adjustments to the things which frustrate him in life, he runs the risk of moving over into the category of neurotic changes. Not all people with neurotic problems have to be institutionalized. In fact, many of them are freely moving within society all the time. However, their problems do become the problems of society in various ways, for their behavior often deviates from that of normal persons. Let's consider four neurotic types.

First, there is *hysteria.* It is demonstrated by wild emotionalism, amnesia, or anesthesia (loss of feeling or sensation). For example, a neurotic person may suffer a loss of memory because of an emotional crisis, and be unable to recall facts needed for making out a necessary report.

Second, there is *neurasthenia.* It is demonstrated by vague aches and pains, or it may take the form of extreme pessimism. For example, a person going through great bereavement over loss of a loved one may develop psychosomatic stomachaches, requiring the help of a psychiatrist more than a medical internist.

Third, there is *psychasthenia.* It is demonstrated by odd weaknesses, obsessions, compulsions, fears and phobias. For example, a soldier assigned to an underground bunker for a tour of duty may suffer from claustrophobia, because of a traumatic experience of being shut in a closet as a child. He has to be assigned to another duty until an analyst can unravel his problem and help him conquer it.

Fourth, there is *anxiety neurosis.* It is demonstrated by an inability to face life as it is and can incapacitate some individuals from living normal lives. For example, a person loaded with charisma is appointed to a high position in a big corporation — but finds his personality alone cannot overcome sniping from every side, so he has a nervous breakdown and has to be treated with tranquilizers and shifted to another position where he has less pressure.

Psychotic Changes

If a person continues in a neurotic state of mind, he runs the risk of moving over into the category of psychotic changes, and this could be the end of the line for him. He will probably have to be institutionalized for his sake and society's sake. Let's consider three psychotic disturbances.

First, there is *schizophrenia.* It is demonstrated by delusions, a retreat from reality, and a possible disintegration of personality. For example, a person may be so psychologically battered and bruised by excessive repression under some tyrannical system that he finds solace only deep within himself. He shuts out his problems, stares continually into space, and cannot be reached by any normal forms of contact made by others around him. He follows no orders, and he has to be tended like a baby for all necessary bodily functions.

Second, there is *manic depression.* It is demonstrated by alternating periods of excited thinking, speaking, and acting, and periods of extreme depression. For example, one day he may be triggered by some small incident into a shouting match and actions requiring forcible restraint, while the next day he may lie on his bed with his face to the wall and want nothing to do with anyone.

Third, there is *paranoia.* It is demonstrated by systematized delusions of persecution on the one hand and power on the other. For example, one day he may walk about furtively, never turning his back to anyone, fearful everybody is out to kill him. The next day he may strut around thinking of himself as some famous world leader and calling on others to pay him the honor and respect he feels he richly deserves.

Although medical science has made much progress in recent years in the development of new drugs, surgical techniques, and therapies designed to help the mentally ill, there are still millions of people who must be closely supervised because of their afflictions. As we would expect, authoritative procedures are much in evidence and very necessary in such situations.

Here we have noted that authority tends to break down in its application to individuals who are finding it difficult to cope with life and its problems. Those making bad adjustments can usually be handled all right, but those who have moved into a neurotic or psychotic state of mind may be beyond self-control and need special treatment.

8

Categories of Control

Three tornadoes ripped through Omaha, Nebraska, in the spring of 1975, destroying 500 homes, damaging 1,000 others, killing 3 people, and injuring 132 others. National Guardsmen were called out to patrol a 3,400-square-block area to prevent looting. Nebraska's Governor J. James Exon surveyed the area and said it was the worst case of property damage in Nebraska's history. It is a sad commentary on our modern society that men with guns had to prevent scavengers from helping themselves to things in the devastated sections of the city. This was a case where government control had to be exercised because certain people would not control themselves.

Lawlessness is rising in our world, and there are many reasons for it. The permissiveness promoted by people who have devised what they call a "new morality" based on "situational ethics" has taken its toll. A general drift away from the fundamental teachings of the Bible and espousal of a vague kind of "humanistic religion" have contributed. Corruption among officials in high places has had its effect. A philosophy of materialism which pushes people into overextending themselves financially has been a factor. The existence of overloaded courts, plea-bargaining, and leniency on hardened criminals cannot be overlooked, plus other factors.

The answer to lawlessness is *control,* and that is what we want to consider here. *Self-control* is what we need most. When that fails, then various forms of common control must be used. In extreme cases, professional help in developing control must be used.

Self-control

Little children lack self-control. That is why they have to be supervised practically every waking moment by all kinds of authorities in their lives. It is the goal of parents, teachers, and others to develop within children some measure of self-control as soon as possible and then increase it as they grow older. If they succeed, then they can be confident these children will be mature and self-disciplined as they move out from under their jurisdiction. If they fail, then they will be fearful of their ability to cope with life's challenges.

We used to hear a lot about such a concept as "strengthening the moral fiber" of a youngster. This implied teaching of standards to the youngster and expectation that he would make those standards his own and live by them. Then along came a new school of thought which said that *indoctrination* was a nasty term, that children should be allowed to express their feelings freely, that authorities should not inhibit that free expression, and that there was no such thing as sin and, therefore, no need for salvation from it. They made *control* and *punishment* nasty terms, too, so that parents and teachers found themselves feeling powerless to exercise their authority over youngsters. They were supposed to convince immature individuals to accept their standards only by example and persuasion.

It is time we came to the realization that as lofty as these ideals may seem to be, they have not been adequate to get the job done. We need to return to the basic truth that self-discipline must be *taught,* as well as *caught,* or we will raise another generation of youngsters who are unsure of what they should think or do.

This whole matter has spiritual implications, too. We may be sure that children must learn obedience to earthly authorities before they will learn obedience to God Himself. The idea that they should be allowed to grow up before choosing their religion just is not feasible. They need to learn about God and His demands upon them while they are still young. If they choose to depart from these things after they mature, at least they have something from which to depart, but the promise of Proverbs 22:6 still can be claimed:

Train up a child in the way he should go: and when he is old, he will not depart from it.

The training has to be the right kind, of course.

Common Control

Where self-control is lacking, various types of *common control* must be substituted. Authorities of different sorts play their roles in the lives of all of us. They may be so common that we hardly even think of them in that way. From the elevator operator who orders us to step to the back, to our employer who governs our activities forty or more hours a week, we take the exercise of authority in our lives for granted. Strange as it may seem, we might be called "the most regimented people in history," for we have a fast-paced way of life and many controls placed upon it.

When we stop to analyze the situation, we probably would not want it any other way. When we make plane reservations, we expect to be told when to report, where to get on board, and when to tighten our seat belts. This makes everything efficient and gives us a sense of security. We don't think of such instructions as oppressive or limiting our freedom. Common control merges with self-control at such a time as that.

One of the strange developments on modern secular college campuses has been the establishment of coed dormitories, in which single male and female students share not only the same buildings, but also the same floors, and even the same rooms. Although it is claimed that brother-sister relationships are generated in this way, more intimate relationships obviously are generated and immorality is widespread. The fact this is permitted in tax-supported schools, in spite of opposition from people of high moral standards, makes it all the worse. Private Christian colleges provide common controls for their students, in order to bolster self-control among them. The rules and regulations governing dormitory life serve a good purpose.

The philosophy underlying common controls is that children, young people, and even adults are either incapable or unwilling always to do what is right for themselves or right for society, so they need help in adhering to proper standards. There are two main sources of standards among men. One is *God and His Holy Word*, which actually is an extension of Himself. The other is *society itself*. The divine standard remains constant, but the societal standard changes according to people, place, time, and circumstances. It is interesting that many of the laws governing society are drawn from God's Word, especially the Ten Commandments. God's law is always right, but man's law sometimes isn't. However, both are designed to help people live as they should.

Professional Control

Where self-control is lacking, and where common controls do not seem to do what we expect of them, we are forced to seek help from those who are specially trained to deal with mental and emotional disorders, which cause individuals to avoid responding to self-control or common controls. These include psychologists, psychiatrists, analysts, and other types of professional counselors. Whatever control they exert comes from their ability to convince disturbed persons that their thinking is twisted and needs to become straightened out again. It all comes back to the basic need for self-control.

Christians should be concerned that only the right kind of professionals be allowed to influence the disturbed among them. If a secular counselor questions the faith of his patient, or gives him advice which is contrary to scriptural standards, he can do more harm than good.

Consider the case of survivors of the Arab guerrilla attack on the Israeli community of Ma'alot in 1974. When the incident ended, the three guerrillas and 22 of the 100 students they had held hostage were dead, and every other student was wounded in some way. Afterward, psychiatrists descended upon the survivors to give them advice. Although the school involved was very religious, and standards were strict, the psychiatrists encouraged the students to smoke cigarettes and seek comfort in sexual companionship, if they wanted to do so. The headmaster of the school, Yosef Genness, said the psychiatrists caused more damage than their advice was worth. When he scolded students for smoking or pinching girls they replied, "The psychiatrist told me it's okay."

Professional counselors do case studies to determine the backgrounds of their patients, seeking for clues which would explain current deviant behavior. The counselors know how to ask leading questions which probe the inner thoughts and feelings the patients may have. There are various tests which they can administer to help analyze the causes of disturbances. A psychiatrist (who must be a medical doctor before he can qualify as a psychiatrist) can also consider any medical problems his patients may have. In some cases, excellent results are produced, while in others the results are minimal. The workings of the mind are still mysterious and unfathomable in many ways.

To summarize: we have analyzed the categories of control used to govern the lives of people. Self-control is obviously our prime concern, but we support it with various forms of common controls and by professional counseling when necessary.

9

Influence of Backgrounds

What does an ex-president of a nation do when he leaves office? Hector Campora was president of Argentina for only six weeks in the spring of 1973. Then he stepped down to allow the reelection of Juan Peron. He was appointed ambassador to Mexico, served in that post until June 1974, and then decided to stay on in Mexico. The right-wing extremist group known as the Argentina Anti-Communist Alliance back in Buenos Aires accused Campora of allowing infiltration of the Peronist movement by Marxist influence and placed his name on a death list. Campora set up a dental clinic in Mexico City, and went back to his original profession, far away from his homeland.

It is natural for anyone to fall back on what he has known in the past, especially if new ventures do not prove to be rewarding. Now we want to think about how a person's background is formed. The purpose: to show the relationships between backgrounds and responses to various types of authority.

Are some persons born with a lawless, untameable nature within them? Does the kind of environment a child or young person has predetermine whether he will be law-abiding or not? Do the decisions an adult makes regarding vocation, location, life-style, and other factors mold his attitudes toward authority? Such questions could call for very complicated answers, but we will try to keep them as simple as possible. Since there is room for considerable latitude, we will also try to refrain from being overly dogmatic.

Inherited Background

The behavioral sciences are not really sure just how much an individual's personality is determined by physical inheritance from his parents or other ancestors. While some would argue that certain mental or emotional traits are passed on, along with physical characteristics, through the genes, others would consider such transference as negligible or nonexistent. Experiments are extremely difficult to set up, for most children grow up under their parents' care and pattern themselves in many ways after them. Control groups would have to be formed from children separated from their parents at birth. Identical twins would provide the best subjects, but who would have the heart to separate them if they could possibly stay together?

If we see the son of an angry man act in an angry manner, we are quick to say he is "a chip off the old block," and cannot help himself; but the fact is that the boy probably picked up that trait at home through imitation. If a man is reckless about obeying driving regulations, and his son is, too, we hear some people comment that there is "bad blood" in the family which causes the offspring to act that way.

If mental and emotional characteristics are inherited, then it is difficult to explain how the child of a lawless parent, or of a set of lawless parents, may turn out to be gentle, teachable, and law-abiding. Did he inherit these traits from a grandparent? The subject seems to raise more questions than can be answered with the present knowledge available.

The general consensus seems to be that little credence can be placed on inherited characteristics, although the door should be left open for future discoveries which might prove otherwise. Certainly there is scientific proof to show that close inbreeding has produced defective offspring in some cases, and someday we may have proof that indicates other factors influence the basic mental and emotional equipment children have at birth.

Environmental Background

Most researchers in personality development would agree that there is no doubt that an individual's environment makes indelible marks upon him. From the day he is born to the day he moves out from under parental supervision, he is bombarded with impressions which are bound to shape and mold his life. As the child grows and begins to enlarge his scope of operations, he is also influenced by neighborhood, school, church, and other environments outside the home. By later adolescence, many have had a part in making his personality what it is, either for good or bad.

It would seem that a wholesome environment would produce good personalities, and an unwholesome environment would produce bad personalities. Here we run into the problem of trying to define what wholesome and unwholesome environments are or what good and bad personalities are. We tend to resort to the usual stereotypes which have served us in the past.

We think of a wholesome environment as one in which upright parents raise their tractable children in pleasant surroundings—where housing, schools, churches, shopping, and recreational facilities are adequate, and there is a general atmosphere of law and order. We think of an unwholesome environment as one in which sleazy parents raise their devious children in substandard surroundings, where the various facilities are deteriorating or lacking altogether, and there is a general atmosphere of lawlessness.

However, reality forces us to note that many variables

can be found which produce exceptions to these stereotypes. Crime may flourish in the slums and ghetto areas,
but it is possible to find parents living there who carefully supervise their children and help them avoid being
pulled into the whirlpool of sin which would drag them
down. Lawful behavior may be the general rule in a
high-class suburban area, but it is certainly not immune
to alcoholism, drug-abuse, rampant immorality, and
other problems which make every day a challenge to
righteous living. As noted previously, statistics show that
crime is increasing in suburbia and exurbia at an aston-
ishing rate.

Anyone would be foolish to deny that certain environments produce adverse influences on individuals
within them, whereas other environments produce helpful influences on those within them, but each environment has to be judged on its own merits. For example,
one might assume that children raised in a poverty-
stricken community in the back hills of Appalachia
would have little opportunity for happiness or financial
success. However, the very circumstances in which they
are raised might determine otherwise. Living in a tightly
knit town, where the work ethic is promoted, such individuals can learn lessons in initiative and perseverance
which youngsters in more affluent communities elsewhere would not learn. Aided by scholarships and work-
study programs, they may be superior in the competitive

labor market and rise rapidly to affluence because they are determined to have it better than their parents did.

Acquired Background

We cannot divorce a person from his inherited characteristics or his environmental background, but for the sake of analysis, let's consider what might be called his *acquired background*. Let's think of a young adult of thirty years of age, who has been away from home for ten years. During that time he has been free to develop his own life with a minimum of interference from his parents or other relatives and friends. Using his technological training in junior college, he has secured a good job, married, had two children, bought a house, and become active in church and community affairs. All the things which have happened to him during that decade constitute his acquired background.

Let's think of another young adult thirty years of age, who had a similar background to the first man mentioned, but who goes in another direction at the age of twenty. He had turned his back on the field for which he was trained in junior college, tried and failed at many jobs, sought comfort in alcohol, and ended up a derelict on skid row. All the things which have happened to him during that decade constitute his acquired background.

It is not difficult to imagine that the first man is going

to be far more responsive to divine authority and societal authority than the second man. The notion that what an individual does with his own life is his own business, so long as he doesn't bother anyone else, is based on a false premise. Each individual *does* influence others for either good or ill. It is illogical and unfair to suppose that what he does is isolated.

Too many individuals today blame their inherited or environmental backgrounds and excuse themselves for their acquired backgrounds. We need to stress the fact that they are personally responsible for overcoming past handicaps and capitalizing on past advantages. Neither God nor society should be accused of failure to give them opportunity to make something good of themselves. God certainly will help them, if they seek His help, and society has many offers to make, even if it is not perfect.

The burden of this chapter has been to show that it is only within a framework of divine and societal authority that an individual can find significance for his existence and become successful at utilizing whatever kind of backgrounds he may have. Compensating for his weaknesses, and making good use of his strengths, he can always improve himself and be a blessing to God and his fellowmen.

10

Moment of Truth

If Cambodia's 7.5 million people thought that their lives would return to normal after the Khmer Rouge victory ended five years of warfare, they were in for a rude awakening. Their "moment of truth" arrived immediately after the takeover, when half of them were uprooted and marched into the interior of the country. Beautiful Phnom Penh was emptied, even to patients in its hospitals, who had to travel as best they could, some on crutches and some crawling. The Communists planned to develop the country on an agrarian economy, and this evidently explained the resettlement of half its population.

Here was a stark example of a totalitarian authority forcing people to come to a drastic decision, and with no advance notice. In most people's lives, however, circumstances which bring people to a "moment of truth" are usually more gradual and involve their making a decision, rather than one being made for them against their will.

The stages involved in making changes in our lives are well known, but it might be helpful to review them here. First, of course, must come an *awareness* of the need to make a change, something often repressed for long periods of time. Second, there will often be *resistance to change*, supported by solid reasoning or even rationalization. Third, there will be the *decision to change*, either by force or by voluntary action. In some cases the changes may be regretted, but in others they will be accepted as valuable.

Awareness of Need

Awareness of the need to make a change may begin with God or with earthly authorities, but it eventually must become a personal matter. In the case of little children or mental incompetents, all decisions may have to be made for them, but with normally developing individuals there are challenges every day which demand that they make personal decisions themselves.

Awareness of the need to change grows out of inherent urges to satisfy various drives built into every person. Physically, he wants to satisfy such needs as eating, drinking, resting, exercising muscles, avoiding excessive heat or cold, and other bodily needs. Mentally, he wants to learn by use of his senses, by reasoning, and, in the case of believers, by revelation. Emotionally, he wants to feel secure, give and get affection, have new experiences, and be free from guilt-complexes. Spiritually, he wants to be reconciled to his Creator, live righteously among his fellowmen, and be sure of a blessed destiny.

A list of needs growing out of a person's physical, mental, emotional, and spiritual urges would be endless. Combine his with those of everyone else around him, and it is no wonder that life becomes extremely complicated sometimes. Each individual is trying to satisfy his needs at the same time, and conflicts naturally develop. Satan wants to cultivate dissension, so he plays one off against the other, taking advantage of everyone he can. According to the Apostle Paul, we should not let Satan take advantage of us, ". . . for we are not ignorant of his devices" (2 Corinthians 2:11).

Awareness of a need to change can lead to confusion and frustration, for people are often fearful of making changes. They are anxious about moving from what they know to what is unknown. A person facing open-heart surgery, for example, may know the need for it but still wonder if the risk is worth it. A student facing an examination may know he has not studied enough but convince himself he has. A bride-to-be may realize she is planning to marry the wrong man, and yet be unwilling to break the engagement and wait for the right one. A sinner may know he needs to surrender to Christ —but be afraid his friends will mock him. This brings us to the problem of resistance to change.

Resistance to Change

Change has become more and more a factor in our modern way of life. It has been brought on by various factors, only some of which will be mentioned here. Scientific research and the resultant technologies based upon it have proliferated so rapidly that more has been done along this line in the twentieth century than in all the previous centuries of man's history. Commercial interests have developed what is called "planned obsolescence" of products in an attempt to get customers to get new models of automobiles and appliances every two or three years. Government bureaucracies seeking to justify their existence have bound us up in reams of red tape. Modern communication systems are so efficient they can tell us what is happening all over the world every day. Modern air travel is so swift that passengers between continents suffer from jet lag. Efficiency experts make careers out of telling people how to change the ways they do things to what are supposed to be better ways.

Western culture has been particularly responsive to change, figuring that something new just has to be better than something old. The evolutionary hypothesis has persuaded most people that change is always in the direction of improvement. Other cultures resisted the concept that "change is progress" for a while, but pressures to conform seemed irresistible. In even the most underdeveloped countries on earth, the new technologies are moving in fast, especially in and around the principal cities.

In other words, change has become so common that it has taken on an aura of rightness. To buck the trend to change is considered as being negative and unprogressive. Threats are made that those who do this will be left behind in the "backwash of history." As an ally of natural curiosity, the pressure to conform to whatever is new has pushed people into many things they might better have avoided. A backlash may develop which will cause people to look more to the past than to the future.

In the midst of all this ferment, individuals continue to make personal decisions day by day regarding their own needs. It would appear that in the material, physical, and mental realms of life, people are quite ready to make changes. However, in the emotional, social, and spiritual realms of life there is more resistance to change.

It is typical of modern man to trade automobiles often, submit to a physician's treatment for an illness, and embrace new ideas learned through the mass media. On the other hand, he may be quite resistant to overcoming a violent temper, going out of his way to make friends in a different social class from his own, and yielding to the Lordship of Christ in his business dealings. It would seem that the things which really are the most important are the ones which change the most slowly, and perhaps that is the way it should be, provided that changes made in those areas are sincere and lasting.

Decision to Change

Awareness of the need to change and resistance to making it may take a long time to develop, but the decision to go ahead and make the change usually comes quickly. This is what is most often referred to as the "moment of truth," for in that moment the full impact of all that has happened up to this point is felt most keenly.

In some cases the decision to change comes because of pressure brought by some form of divine or earthly authority. The individual involved finally realizes that he actually has little choice in the matter, so that the decision is virtually made for him. In other cases the decision to change comes entirely from the person's own voluntary action. His will decides it will be so, and it is done.

Once the decision is firm, the next step is implementation. For example, the college graduate who has applied to and been accepted by both a law school and a medical school must now determine which graduate program he will enter. Once committed, his life will probably go in a direction far different from the other he contemplated. All the details involved in entering the advanced program will require his full attention from then on.

There is always the possibility that even a voluntary decision to make a change in one's life will be regretted afterward. In time that regret may fade away, but it could also grow. Depending on how involved the change was, he might be able to go back and resume a previous role, but it often is impossible to really turn backward. He makes the adjustments necessary and keeps going forward.

There are many pitfalls in everyone's path, some accidental and some deliberate. All types of human authorities can give a person bad advice, which might cause serious problems. That's why it is vitally important for everyone to seek the will of God for every step he takes. The Lord is all-wise, and He never gives counsel which is detrimental to those who sincerely ask His help.

Let us not fear those "moments of truth" when they come to us. Instead, let us see in them opportunities for God to give us direction. If we take time to think through all the implications, ask God in prayer to guide us, and receive the assurance of His will and the peace which always accompanies it, we can make the right decisions. A helpful passage on this subject is Philippians 4:6-9.

11

Classes of Counseling

Benjamin Cummings, four, a foster child living in the Auburn-Elmwood section of Buffalo, New York, wandered away from home around 5 P.M. one Monday. His foster mother, Mrs. Nicholas Mortellaro, notified the police, and they enlisted the aid of the K-9 Corps. A multitude of neighbors heard about the lost boy and helped comb the streets and alleys of the area. Benjamin was located not far away and returned to his home about 1 A.M. the next morning. During the eight hours he was missing, Mrs. Mortellaro was overwhelmed by the concern people showed for her problem.

This is the way most problems are solved. Individuals receive advice and help from relatives, friends, and various government or private agencies. We might refer to this as the *informal category* of counseling. Those who require special help can take advantage of individual or group therapy with trained counselors in private practice or those connected with mental health clinics sponsored by government agencies or charitable organizations. We might refer to this as the *out-patient category* of formal counseling. In cases where individuals cannot cope with life, and they become dangerous to themselves and others, twenty-four-hour care may be required, including specialized counseling and therapy. We might refer to this as the *institutional category* of formal counseling.

Informal Class

Practically every time two individuals interact with each other, some form of counseling takes place. In certain cases this is preventive in nature or takes the form of warnings. One traveler will tell another traveler to avoid certain stretches of bad road, or one gardener will warn another of the bad side effects of a particular pesticide. Some counseling is curative in nature or takes the form of problem-solving. One parent will tell another parent how he succeeded in getting his children to come home on time. One housewife will tell another how she got berry stains out of her carpet.

Much of the informal counseling which goes on among

relatives, close friends, and sometimes even casual acquaintances is centered on dealing with the various types of maladjustments we considered in the first part of chapter 7—*rationalization, compensation* (or substitution), *identification, compromise, repression, regression, withdrawal,* and *negativism* (or egocentrism). It may be that some people would go to trained counselors for help with these, but the majority probably would not. If they become aware that any of these is a problem, they will usually try to find a solution themselves or ask help from other nonprofessionals around them.

King Solomon wrote, "Where no counsel is, the people fall: but in the multitude of counsellors there is safety" (Proverbs 11:14). However, he did not mean that all counsel is helpful. "The thoughts of the righteous are right: but the counsels of the wicked are deceit" (12:5). Therefore, although we are to seek out the counsel of others, we must make sure they think God's thoughts and are not motivated by Satan in what they say. The Apostle John said, ". . . try the spirits whether they are of God: because many false prophets are gone out into the world" (1 John 4:1). Anyone guided by the Holy Spirit will give good counsel, but anyone under the influence of evil spirits will give bad counsel.

One of the mistakes people often make is that they consider their problems to be identical with those of others, so they think solutions others found will also apply in their own cases. However, it is unlikely that they or their situations are exactly like those of others, and the solutions others used may not work with them. Each person has to realize he is unique and then seek to know God's will for himself.

Out-patient Class

Although there is still some stigma attached to undergoing psychological or psychiatric treatment, the old attitudes are slowly changing. In fact, among the famous and rich there is a certain sophistication in having oneself under analysis. Professional counselors often command high fees for their services and are among the elite in a community. With articles, books, lectures, and other means they enhance both their reputations and incomes.

There are, of course, various programs which offer mental health services to people of limited incomes, too. These are sponsored by government agencies or charitable organizations. Information about them can usually be obtained by contacting one's city or county health department. A wide range of problems—from emotional disturbances among children to marriage conflicts among adults—are handled by experts in the various fields.

Group-therapy sessions have been found helpful in some cases. Individuals having similar problems get together under the leadership of a trained counselor and get their feelings out into the open. By sharing and by group pressure, an individual sometimes finds it possible to get relief from nagging problems. At least he will realize he is not alone as far as struggling with his particular kind of problems is concerned. Realizing others have been successful in finding deliverance, he is encouraged to find it as well. This is one of those instances in which group discipline may operate, and sometimes peer pressure is exactly what a person needs, rather than imposition of authority by someone above him.

The use of new drugs by mental health physicians has opened up tremendous possibilities for out-patient treatment in modern times. Many individuals who once had to be institutionalized continuously are now able to pursue fairly normal lives out in society, if they will faithfully take their medications. Thus, *chemical therapy* is added to *psychological therapy* to help those suffering from mental and emotional problems.

The role of the pastor as a counselor ought not to be overlooked at this point. Spiritual counsel is important in treating the needs of people. In some cases, spiritual treatment is all that is needed, while in other cases, it serves in a supportive role to physical, psychological, or psychiatric treatment. *Pastors really ought to have spe-*

*cial training in counseling techniques, or even they can
do more harm than good.* In cases of neurotic or psychotic behavior, they should refer their parishioners to
professionals trained to handle such aberrations.

Institutional Class

Those afflicted by serious mental and emotional problems will likely have to be placed in institutions. It has
been estimated that this will involve one out of every
ten people alive today at one point or another during
their lives. With some, of course, lifelong institutional
care is required.

Mental hospitals are not as numerous as regular hospitals, and often they are tucked away in locations not
readily visible from main highways. Once on the
grounds, however, it is evident they are well populated
and often very large—almost like cities by themselves.
It has been estimated that there are as many people in
mental hospitals as there are in regular hospitals. This
is due in part to the fact that care of mental patients
normally requires longer periods of time than care of
patients with physical problems.

It would be unfair to liken mental hospitals today to
the so-called snake pits of the past, but facilities and
care do range widely from one part of the country to
another. Those which have low budgets, or staffs which

are careless, naturally cannot provide the kind of service offered by those which are well financed and staffed by dedicated workers.

One of the handicaps of treatment in a mental institution is that a patient is put into daily contact with other patients who also have mental or emotional problems. It might be argued that aberrations have a contagious quality, and some have thought this affected staff members, as well as patients, over extended periods of time. Some patients are permitted temporary releases, so they have opportunities to be with loved ones, friends, and people in normal society, and this has therapeutic value.

Authorities who release patients from mental hospitals shoulder a grave responsibility. They receive little or no acclaim from the general public for those they return to society cured and able to assume normal patterns of life; but they are severely criticized if they release someone who breaks down again and perhaps commits a heinous crime. It is impossible to have a foolproof system of evaluation regarding those to be released, so the public will just have to accept the fact that occasionally there will be unfortunate incidents traceable to premature releases.

Here we have sought to describe briefly the wide range of counseling which goes on continuously in our world. From the friendly advice offered by an acquaintance regarding some mundane matter to the highly skilled analysis and treatment of a severely disturbed patient in a mental hospital, there are all kinds of counseling activities in operation. Authority is most evident among those who have to be institutionalized, of course, for they cannot be held responsible for themselves, either in part or in whole, and must be closely supervised.

12

Principles of Counseling

During the Arab-Israeli War of 1967, the Egyptians sank vessels in the Suez Canal, and it remained blockaded for the next eight years. Fourteen large ships were trapped by this and had to be maintained by skeleton crews with the hope the canal would some day be open again. In 1975, after a massive clearance of sunken ships, mines, and other obstructions, two West German cargo ships, the *Munsterland* and her sister ship, the *Nordwind*, finally made the sixty-mile trip northward from Great Bitter Lake to Port Said on the Mediterranean coast. The other twelve ships were to follow later.

The predicament those ships faced might be compared with individuals who are bottled up by problems and who may remain that way for years, before experiencing deliverance. It is our goal now to suggest some simple principles anyone of normal intelligence and sensitivity can use to help people with everyday problems

112

find relief from them. This could go a long way toward helping them avoid moving over into a neurotic or psychotic state requiring professional counseling by highly trained experts. (These principles are designed for laymen seeking to help individuals with *routine maladjustments*. Anyone having more serious problems should be referred to mental health authorities for treatment.)

Establishing Rapport

A person playing the role of a counselor needs to make it very clear that he is available to individuals who have problems they would like to discuss with him. He may be a close friend of the troubled person, or he may be only a casual acquaintance or a stranger. The important thing is that he appears ready to listen and will indicate a time and place for conversation.

It is difficult, and sometimes impossible, to counsel a person if there are distractions. That's why it is unwise to attempt to do it in a busy hallway or a crowded room. Moving to a private, quite place will make it easier to establish rapport, hear the problem the person has, and seek a solution for it.

If you are dealing with someone of the opposite sex, and the possibility of scandal is present, certain safeguards may have to be observed. Leaving a door to the room ajar, having a third party in the general vicinity of the room, or meeting in a secluded but public place may be sufficient. A counselor always has to be aware that troubled people sometimes try to find relief from nervous tension by emotional involvement with the counselor, and this should not be allowed to happen.

Establishing rapport with another person may be done quickly in some cases but take a long time in other cases. A troubled person does not always feel free to talk right away. If the counselor remains calm, sympathetic, and unhurried, showing he understands and is willing to wait, the counselee will eventually relax and begin to share what is on his heart and mind.

Determining Problems

As the troubled person begins to talk, he is likely to speak of what are called *surface problems*. He is hesitant to go directly to his main problem, so he works around the periphery, testing out the counselor's reactions. This stage of the interview is important for two reasons: First, it helps the counselee determine whether the counselor can be trusted with a revelation of the big problem. Second, it gives the counselor opportunity to build up a profile of the individual's background and look for clues to what his real problem may be.

For example, consider a man who is an electronics engineer. He might begin by complaining about his employer, his fellow employees, irritating customers, problems involving equipment, locations of jobs for which he is responsible, and various other factors connected with his work. As he talks, the counselor develops a better understanding of this man's background. Clues seem to point to the fact that the man actually ended up in the wrong vocation, but he feels he is so involved now that he cannot make a change to something else. Probing even deeper, it is revealed that as a young man, this engineer, had a call from God for missionary service, but he refused it and has been miserable ever since.

It is an interesting thing that most people who seek counseling already know what their real problems are, and they often also know the solutions to those problems. They come to a counselor to get the courage they need for facing both the problems and their solutions. The counselor serves an important function by acting as a mirror for reflecting back to the counselees what they cannot see objectively for themselves—because they are too wrapped up in their subjective feelings.

There are two reactions to keep in mind as a troubled person gets closer and closer to his real problem, and then finally brings it up to the surface for scrutiny. First, the counselor must realize that the counselee may become quite agitated as he comes to the point of revealing his problem. The counselor must resist the temptation to cut off the discussion and suggest another time to finish it, because if he holds steady the hidden problem is going to be brought out into the open where it can be faced squarely. Second, the counselor must do his best to be shockproof when sordid secrets are unearthed. The degradation of the human heart can produce some terrible things in people, even in those who outwardly appear to be upright and thoroughly respectable members of a community.

Getting a deep-seated problem out into the open can have great cathartic value to a troubled person. He may have allowed it to fester there for days, weeks, months, or even years, and it is a relief to know at least one other person is now aware of it. A counselor may not personally appreciate being the partner of a psychological regurgitation, but he must keep this to himself and commend the counselee for being strong enough to make his problem known.

Encouraging Solutions

Once a counselee's real problem has been determined, the next obvious step is to seek a solution for it. At this point, the counselor assumes a crucial role as an authority in the eyes of the counselee, who may even say he is willing to do anything the counselor suggests. This is flattering to the counselor's ego, and he runs the risk of being carried away with a sense of his own importance. He must resist this and carefully decide how to

handle the situation in the best interests of the counselee.

The first thing he should remember is *to avoid giving
quick advice*. He is tempted to do this in an effort to
soothe the shattered feelings of the troubled person.
There may be many other facts which have to be known
before an adequate solution to the problem can be tried.
The counselee may actually already know what the solution should be, or he may at least have a general idea
of what it should be.

Take the case of the engineer mentioned earlier. He
may have known for years that he ought to offer his
training and experience in electronics to the Lord. It
was a general solution, but it lacked specific applications. Now the counselor might suggest that the engineer consider teaching in a Christian school preparing
young people for the Lord's work, or he might suggest
names and addresses of mission boards the engineer
could contact to see if they could use him in their com-
munications programs somewhere in foreign lands. He
no doubt would have to give up a high salary to do
this, but he could finally find the happiness which has
eluded him for many years.

Occasionally a counselor will meet a person who has
been so dominated by others all his life, that even as
an adult, he does not realize he has the right to self-
direction for his life. As a result, he has made it a habit
to lean on the wisdom and strength of others for prob-

lems big and small. The reason he comes to the counselor for help indicates that he is following this pattern. That means the counselor will have to carefully convince this person that he has to learn to make his own decisions and follow through on them with God's help.

The Christian who counsels others has something to offer which secular counselors do not have. He can take time to pray with the counselee that God will help him face both his problem and the solution for it with courage. Even after they have separated, the counselor can make this a matter for daily prayer. If the counselee is successful in solving his problem, the counselor can praise the Lord for answering prayer and suggest that the counselee do this as well.

Here we have taken a look at simple counseling principles which anyone with normal maturity and intelligence can use to help those who are troubled. To summarize: first, an effort must be made to establish rapport with the counselee, so he trusts the counselor and will share his thoughts and feelings with him. Second, surface problems must be dealt with and the real problem revealed. Third, the counselor must help the counselee face both his problem and its solution with courage, depending on the Lord all the way.

Counseling is a ministry which might not receive much publicity, but it can produce wonderful results in the lives of troubled people.

13

Benefits of Order

The breakdown of authority increases as the breakdown
of morality continues. Policemen can never maintain
law and order by themselves. They must have the support of the general public. Consider the case of Steven
Laine, director of public affairs for Agriculture Secre-
tary Earl L. Butz in Washington, D.C.

On Human Kindness Day, Laine was walking among
a crowd of 125,000 gathered near the Washington Mon-
ument for a day of rock music sponsored by the park
service. He was attacked from behind and stabbed in
the right eye. He called for help, but no one responded,
and he had to walk to a first-aid station by himself.
Doctors who later examined him said he would lose the
eye. Park police said about 100 persons reported being

robbed or assaulted that day. It was some way to celebrate human kindness, wasn't it?

In chapter 3 consideration was given to the blessings of conformity. The emphasis there was primarily on the personal level. Now we will take a look at the benefits of order on a societal level. We want to be realistic about prospects for the future, and there are many disquieting indications that anarchy may become widespread. On the other hand, the vast majority of people have a deep desire for order, and hope peace can come to this globe. We can be idealistic to the extent that we see in God and His Word the possibility of true peace through spiritual regeneration. No matter how difficult earthly circumstances become, we must remain anchored to that hope.

Specter of Anarchy

The breakdown of authority has become a pervasive fact of life in our times. The twentieth century began with clashes between management and labor which were often violent and bloody, leading to legislation which was designed to promote peaceful negotiations. Over eighty American cities felt the sting of race riots in the sixties, leading to legislation designed to end discrimination. Protest marches to end the war in Vietnam sometimes turned into riots. Almost every decade has found war going on in such countries as China, Korea,

Vietnam, Cambodia, Laos, Israel, Egypt, Syria, Nigeria, Cuba, India, Pakistan, Bangladesh, and most of the nations of Europe. During times of warfare there are usually periods of anarchy as governments change hands.

Some people wonder if we are approaching a state of affairs which described the situation in ancient Israel: "In those days there was no king in Israel: every man did that which was right in his own eyes" (Judges 21:25). That should not be used as a proof-text for a monarchial form of government. The point is that it showed what happened when there was a lack of leadership. It seems to support the concept that even poor leadership is better than no leadership at all.

An incident which took place during Paul's third missionary journey showed that pagan leadership was beneficial at the city of Ephesus, located on the western coast of Asia Minor (Turkey). Demetrius and his guild of silversmiths were so concerned about the impact of the Gospel and its effect on their sale of miniature silver shrines of the goddess Artemis (Diana) that they stirred up a riot. Rushing into the amphitheater, the crowd chanted and howled for two hours. Finally, the executive officer of the city assembly (town clerk), a magistrate of great authority, quieted the people down. He said any complaints against the Christians would have to be decided in a lawful assembly, and then he dispersed the crowd (*see* Acts 19:23-41).

The administrative leadership of the United States

underwent sudden change in the early seventies. The vice-president resigned after pleading "no contest" to charges of accepting kickbacks from contractors in Maryland. The president resigned after disclosures of cover-ups in the Watergate scandal. That was unprecedented in American history, and so was the fact that the two top leaders who replaced them were put into office without being elected by the people. However, the system survived, even if the top leadership did not.

There are nearly two hundred sovereign nations in the world today. Many of them are so unstable that they are regularly overturned by military coups or even by university students. Guerrilla forces are often involved. The chaos which results from revolutions brings untold hardship to millions of people caught in the middle. Many accounts of atrocities are never publicized.

Are men on a treadmill to oblivion? Many discouraging factors would indicate this is so. The pace of life grows faster, with all the stresses and strains that induces. The world's population expands, and its resources diminish, meaning struggles are bound to occur. Secularistic, atheistic philosophies now control the thinking of millions, and their influence is spreading. Devastating weapons now in existence could make the holocausts described in Revelation literally possible in our day. Erosion of morality is so widespread that some fear it cannot be restored again. Satan is preparing the world for the rule of the Antichrist (*see* 2 Thessalonians 2:3-12).

Desire for Order

Amidst all the pronouncements of gloom and doom, however, there are other factors we should keep in mind. The vast majority of people have a deep desire for order in the world. It is normally the leaders who become intoxicated with power, not the common people. As the lower and middle classes become more affluent, better educated, and more expressive, they are going to demand more stability. That means they will call for law and order.

We see signs of this now. One of the interesting developments is that calls for law and order are coming from both the extreme right and from the extreme left. We expected it from the hard-line conservatives on the right, but we are surprised to hear it from the hard-line liberals on the left. This would seem to say to us that the value of law and order is recognized by authorities of all persuasions, except for outright anarchists, and if they came to power they would likely recognize it, too.

 We must not overlook the fact that Jesus declared righteous believers to be "the salt of the earth" and "the light of the world" (*see* Matthew 5:13-16). Followers of Christ have always permeated society with their beliefs and practices, and they will continue to do so until He comes back to translate them to heaven. No matter how bad the world becomes, that faithful remnant in every generation will have its influence on other men.

Perhaps even a selfish motive will help promote law and order. As the people of earth steadily improve their living standards, they will have more and more to lose in the absence of law and order. Therefore, it would seem logical to assume they will demand stable living conditions and punishment of those who would destroy law and order.

Hope of Peace

Two international organizations have tried to bring about world peace — but without success. They were the League of Nations, following World War I, and the United Nations, following World War II. Billions of dollars have been poured into actions for maintaining peace, but men's sinful natures prevailed.

Is the world heading for one government in the years ahead? Will sovereign nations yield up their right to govern themselves in order to merge into one massive government promising to bring peace and prosperity to the whole earth? Some indications would seem to point in that direction. When it happens, it will be under the leadership of the Antichrist. In the early stage of its development, a general delusion will engulf mankind, so that the lies of the Antichrist will be accepted as truths (*see* 2 Thessalonians 2:11). Even the Jews will be deceived, and the Antichrist will make a covenant with them. However, he will break that covenant and usher in the great tribulation period (*see* Daniel 9:27; Revelation 13:1-18). The hope of peace will be shattered for men on earth.

However, deliverance will come from heaven, for Christ will come back to earth with His hosts and destroy the Antichrist and his armies at the Battle of Armageddon (*see* 2 Thessalonians 2:8; Revelation 14:14-20; 19:11-19). The Antichrist will be slain and he will be consigned to the lake of fire (*see* Daniel 7:11; Revelation 19:20).

Now the greatest Authority of all will set all things straight. The nations will appear before Christ to be judged (*see* Matthew 25:31-46). Jerusalem will become the capital of His worldwide kingdom (*see* Psalms 98:9; Isaiah 2:2, 3; 11:9; Micah 4:2, 3; Zechariah 8:20-23; 14:9). Even wild animals will become tame (*see* Isaiah 11:6-8; 65:25). Peace will come because the Prince of Peace returns (*see* Isaiah 9:6, 7).

In the meantime, how are we to keep our hope of peace alive? We must commit ourselves to God and try to get others to do the same. Peace *with* God comes through faith in Christ as our personal Saviour from sin (*see* Romans 5:1). The peace *of* God comes through trusting Him in all situations (*see* Philippians 4:6, 7).

Peace with our fellowmen comes through overcoming evil with goodness (*see* Romans 12:17-21; Hebrews 12:14). In spite of harsh circumstances, we can rejoice in the God of our salvation (*see* Habakkuk 3:17-19; Philippians 4:4).

Our hope for time and eternity is in Him!

DATE DUE